Psychic Deve

A Practical Guide to

Ps~~ychic Gifts~~

Emily Stroia

"Intuition is seeing with the soul."
— Dean Koontz

Dedicated to Spirit for always being guiding me and showing me the light even in times of darkness & to Baba for looking down on us from above.

Infinite Love & Gratitude

Sign up for Emily's Newsletter to receive a Free Bonus Psychic Gift!

Table of Contents

Foreword

Thank you for purchasing my book! I am so excited to be a part of this journey with you. Learning about your psychic gifts is like tapping into an invisible world within and outside of yourself. It can be overwhelming, exciting and magical all at the same time! I was always really intuitive growing up but never thought to develop my gifts until I was a young adult. I never knew there was so much information about psychic development until I took a class for it.

As I continued to study, everything that I once questioned about my intuition became clear. It was as if a lightbulb went off and I realized I did have a sixth sense about things. I hope to give that to you with this book, those "A-HA!" moments where you will recognize your intuition and become more aware of it.

I have studied this work extensively and continue to study and teach psychic development to my students and clients. I believe we all have the power to tap into our intuition and can use it for personal guidance. It's all in how we decide to listen to it.

Feel free to sign up for my newsletter to receive a free iTunes podcast and updates on upcoming eBooks, discounts and events! Sending you positive light on your own spiritual journey.

Introduction: Our 6th Sense_

What does it mean to be 'psychic'? Do we really have a sixth sense or an intuition? The word psychic is derived from the Greek *psukhikos* then translated to English around the early 19th century as *psyche* meaning 'the human soul, mind or spirit'.

This word has been glamourized by popular media, Hollywood and entertainment and usually what comes to mind for most people are tarot card readers, crystal balls, turbans and fancy shops on the corners of sidewalks. At least that's what came to my mind for me before I realized and understood my gift.

I always heard the phrases "Listen to your gut. Trust your instincts. Follow your intuition." But I never truly understood what that meant. Most times I did just go with my first feeling about something and if I didn't get a good vibe, I listened.

The sense of mysticism and symbolism has been a running theme in my family before I was even born. I remember my Dad sharing his dreams of spirit communication with my grandmother and premonitions of things to come before they happened. My grandmother was also known to be an intuitive and possessed a sixth sense about things. I naturally embraced this connection to my intuition and allowed it to be my compass for life.

Why would anyone want to develop their intuition? For one, it helps you to make better life decisions.

Intuition is there to serve as your spiritual GPS to guide and provide insight to lessons needed to learn, patterns of behavior to break and new perspectives on the overall bigger picture.

What does intuitive really mean? Is everyone intuitive or psychic? I personally believe we all have this gift of intuition. It's an inner knowing without reason or logic to explain all the details.

Have you ever met someone and immediately sensed something was off? This happens all the time in love, life and career. Many times clients have come in saying they met someone on a date and got a 'bad vibe' and discovered later their gut feeling was right.

There are other classic examples of our intuition interacting with us such as when a favorite song randomly pops in our head and then we hear it on the radio.

I believe as children we are much more sensitive and aware to our intuition.

As adults we've been conditioned to ignore our "inner voice" and go with logic instead. There is a magic in being able to trust that feeling without understanding why. With time we see why it was important to go with that gut feeling.

Not everything in our lives will follow a logical step-by-step process and most times it doesn't. There may be bumps and detours in the process that force us to reevaluate and often we will need to rely on our intuition to guide us.

As a psychic medium, I've noticed I use my intuition quite often with just about everything. It is as simple as deciding what train to ride for my morning commute to Manhattan or life choices such as the next step in my career.

Intuition is useful for simple daily tasks and can also assist us in life decisions such as interviewing for jobs, career change, relationship concerns, family issues, health, relocation and more.

My goal with this book is to provide you with knowledgeable material and practical exercises that will help you in your exploration of psychic development. I hope to leave you feeling more inspired and aware of that inner voice inside us all, our intuition.

Chapter 1

The Difference between a Psychic & a Medium

Psychic and medium are interchangeably used all the time in the media and movies. But what is actually the difference between both?

A psychic is able to tune into the energy field of a place, person, area/ building or object. They can also pick up on current events, the past and see possible future outcomes.

A medium is able to connect with passed loved ones and provide evidential details about the deceased. A medium may be able to verify details such as how a person died, type of passing, age, personality, job occupation, married/single, kids, favorite hobbies, memories and a message.

Can a psychic be a medium? A psychic may also be a medium but a medium *must* be psychic because psychic ability is the foundation to any type of mediumship. However not all psychics will make strong mediums and not all mediums will make very good psychics. We all have different gifts and abilities.

Mediums are able to receive impressions from the Spirit World such as connect with passed loved ones and Spirit Guides; higher vibrational beings who continue to work with us by providing wisdom and guidance in our lives. They channel this information through telepathic communication with Spirit.

Psychics will receive impressions from the auric or energy field of a person, place, object or telepathically. They don't usually work with Spirit energy to receive information about someone psychically because they can sense it intuitively.

Psychics and mediums will receive information through their paraphysical or psychic senses such as with clairvoyance, clairaudience or other spiritual faculties (covered in Chapter 3).

Psychic development can assist in a variety of ways including life decisions, finding lost objects, relocation and heighten personal awareness. Mediumship is helpful when we want to connect with passed loved ones for messages or Spirit Guides for life guidance.

As you develop your intuition, you will notice the difference between psychic and mediumship impressions.

Chapter 2

How to Recognize a Psychic Impression

One of the most common questions to psychic development is how can you tell if what you are feeling or receiving is actually psychic, logic or just pure imagination?

Psychic or 'intuitive' impressions are very different from our imagination and logic. These impressions are usually spontaneous or random sensations, thoughts, feelings, images and even sometimes scents or tastes.

They manifest in all types of ways such as gut feelings, premonitions, visions, and past information. A person may get a feeling that something is about to change in their work environment such as potential lay-offs and find out the next morning 10 people were laid off. This would be a psychic impression or our intuition telling us something.

We don't receive these impressions through our five physical senses but through our *paraphysical* senses or the five "clairs" which I will cover in the following chapter.

Merriam-Webster Dictionary defines paraphysical as resembling physical phenomena but without recognizable physical cause.

An example of this is a person may feel as if they smell smoke but there is no physical presence of smoke in the environment. The person may then be receiving a psychic impression of a former fire that occurred in that place.

How can you tell the difference between receiving a psychic impression versus logic?

Psychic Impressions will manifest in the following forms:

· Persistent, nagging impression, out of the blue interruption

· Random or spontaneous

· Interrupts your normal train of thought or being

· Could disagree with your own belief system, example: Going on a date for the first time and suddenly get the urge to have a drink even though you are sober and don't drink alcohol. Later, you find out your date works as a bartender.

· Strong emotion or memory behind it.

· Not triggered by your external environment at all or outside stimulation.

· Reoccurring Visual symbols/numbers such as 1111 or 1212

· Colors/Temperature change

Psychic impressions will be persistent and nag at you. They may also come in out of the blue and interrupt your train of thought.

For example, you are working doing data-entry at your desk when an image of your childhood best friend in deep emotional distress randomly pops up in your mind. You haven't talked to her in years and then feel an urge to Facebook her because you can't ignore the feeling. After logging onto Facebook, you see from her status update that her mother passed away recently.

This is one example of how a psychic impression manifests to get our attention. There is no external environment stimulation and may interrupt your normal thought process or focus of concentration.

Logic usually follows a particular train of thought or pattern and is stimulated by environmental factors or outside circumstances. Our imagination is similar such as having a daydream and then is dismissed shortly after. With psychic impressions the information is much harder to dismiss or ignore.

What type of information can you receive in a psychic impression?

Psychic impressions can provide information about a person, place, object or animal such as:

· The past

· Former relationships

· Family

· Life history

· Milestones in someone's life

· Possible future paths

· Present day circumstances

· Recent life changes

· Hobbies/interests

· Soul lessons or karmic patterns

As you develop your intuition, it is important for your mind to be in a clear, focused and neutral space. Meditation will help to de-clutter your mind to be more aware of psychic impressions and intuition.

Recognize a Psychic Impression Exercise

Take a few deep breaths and get into a comfortable seated position. Scan your body from head to toe for any tension. As you do this, imagine the tension floating away in a bubble and disappearing.

Now imagine a beautiful golden light coming in at the top of your head and expanding down from your crown chakra to your feet connecting you to Mother Earth. This healing light is divine energy and connects you to the Universe, a Higher Source or your Higher Self.

Sit with this energy and allow it to speak to you. You may see or feel sensations that weren't there before. Notice for any impressions that may come out of nowhere. It could be a thought, word, feeling or sensation. You may even see a color or feel a temperature change.

When you are ready, bring yourself back to the room and open your eyes. Write down your experience and notice the difference in how you feel from when you began the exercise. Were there any spontaneous feelings or impressions that came out of nowhere?

Chapter 3

The 5 'Clairs' or Psychic Senses

As you develop your intuition, you will receive impressions, feelings or other sensations in various ways. You've probably heard the terms 'clairvoyant' or 'clairsentient' but what do these words mean?

We go through daily activities and receive spontaneous psychic impressions all the time but may not know it. Sometimes you hear people say they had a gut feeling or vibe about something.

Our intuition is constantly communicating with us but our logic may dismiss these impressions. We have been conditioned to rely less on our natural instincts and more on logic.

So how can we begin to understand if something we receive is actually our intuition versus logic or imagination?

In the same way we experience the world with our five physical senses, we also experience the world intuitively with *paraphysical* senses.

These paraphysical senses are: clairvoyance, clairaudience, clairsentience, clairgustance and clairscent.

Clairvoyance

Clair is the French term for 'clear' and clairvoyance is translated to "clear-seeing" or your "inner-vision".

When you receive a psychic impression through clairvoyance you may subjectively see images, pictures, colors and symbols in your mind's eye or the center of your forehead, right above the brow area.

You will see psychics and mediums shift their eye gaze to an area in a room not because they are staring off into space but because they are receiving a clairvoyant impression in their mind's eye. Clairvoyant impressions are usually described as if seeing an image projected on a blank screen or similar to watching a movie trailer in your mind.

In the beginning people may see fleeting images or receive subtle clairvoyant impressions. With enough focus and concentration the image or impression may last longer and deliver more information.

The images you receive may be a literal or symbolic representations of something.

For example, during a clairvoyant exercise a student was reading for her partner and said she didn't know why all she could see was a palm tree. Her partner then verified the palm tree was a literal symbol of her being from Miami, Florida.

Clairvoyant impressions are more symbolic than literal.

For example, let's say you meet an old friend for coffee and immediately you see a red rose in your mind. The rose could have two meanings. How would you interpret it?

It could literally mean the person's favorite flowers are red roses or symbolically the rose represents a new love interest in their life, relationship energy, or your own interpretation.

The way you receive and interpret information is up to you. There are no right or wrong meanings.

How do you know if you are clairvoyant?

The way we experience the world with our physical senses will reflect in how we receive information through our paraphysical senses. For example, if you are predominantly a very visual person then most likely you would experience clairvoyance predominantly.

People who tend to first remember things visually such as a person's face, photos, famous paintings, nature or anything visually stimulating may be more clairvoyant.

You may also be predominantly clairvoyant if you are a very vivid, detailed dreamer or can visualize a scene in your mind very well. This is often referred to as "daydreaming" in which you can see things clearly in your mind using your imagination.

If you aren't a very visual person it doesn't mean you won't experience clairvoyance at all. As you practice working with clairvoyance you may start to become stronger in it over time.

How can you train or exercise your clairvoyance?

There are several simple ways you can train your clairvoyance. Try the following exercises and   take notes on how you did after. Now is a good time to start a Psychic Journal to document information you receive and your spiritual progress.

Clairvoyance Exercise 1:

This exercise can be done indoors or outdoors. If you can, venture outside and spend time in nature either in a local park, beach or landmark. Visually notice the details of the trees, flowers, and overall scenery around you. Hold these images in your mind concentrating in your third eye or center of your forehead area.

You can even draw what you are looking at or take a photo and paint it later. Painting, drawing, collage, watercolor or any other artistic medium will also help to activate your clairvoyant ability.

Indoors: You can also visit an art museum and do the same process but indoors. Take notice of the pieces in the museum including the color, textures and type of artistic medium used. Feel free to draw a light sketch of it or just hold the piece in your mind for 5-10 seconds.

Clairvoyance Exercise 2: You may want to record a guided audio of this exercise either on a cellphone or any recording device to play it back later.

First, get into a comfortable sitting position with your feet either planted on the ground or crossed with your back straight against a solid surface.

Take three long deep breaths in and exhale slowly releasing any tension held in the body. During this time you may want to scan your body from head-to-toe and relax the muscles in your face, shoulders, legs and feet.

Imagine a ball of shimmering white light in the core of your stomach and with each breath in visualize this white expanding filling your entire being from head-to-toe. Allow yourself to sit with this light and imagine it connecting to a divine energy larger than you.

Now shift your awareness to the center of your forehead, the third eye chakra or clairvoyant energy center. Notice how your third eye feels. Is it open, closed or semi-open? Visualize a clear transparent prism at the center of your third eye. This prism brings forth colors and images for you. What colors do you see? Let the prism tell you a story and take you on a beautiful visual journey.

When you are ready, begin to shift your awareness back to the room and open your eyes. Write down your experience. Don't be disappointed if you weren't able to see much. You are always welcome to practice this exercise every day or whenever to strengthen your clairvoyance.

Clairaudience

The literal translation for clairaudience is "clear-hearing" and often described as our "inner-hearing". *Webster's Dictionary* defines clairaudience as "the power or faculty of hearing something not present to the ear but regarded as having objective reality".

In the same way we physically hear sounds in our waking life, clairaudience is the gift to hear sounds, music, words and voices in our inner ear.

There are two types of clairaudience; objective and subjective. Objective clairaudience occurs in the physical real world where everyone can hear it such as sitting in a séance and hearing the voice of a Spirit Guide communicate to the group.

Subjective clairaudience is only heard in the person's mind, inner ear or psychic ear. The information, voice or sound may come out of nowhere and appear in your mind and can be similar to how you hear sounds in a dream.

For the longest time I was terrified of the clairaudience faculty because of some of the horror stories about people who heard Spirits talking to them at odd hours of the night or worse hearing a voice tell them to hurt someone or themselves.

However, Clairaudience is not to be confused with schizophrenia or mental health conditions where someone would hear voices and be told to hurt themselves or others. Spirit will never tell you to harm another person or yourself. If you are experiencing this or anyone you know is then it is highly recommended they consult a health professional.

I had to learn to trust this ability as a divine gift from my higher self. Your higher self is the purest form of you, your soul essence or intelligence. It knows what is best for you in your spiritual journey as you develop psychically.

Clairaudience is like experiencing a stream of consciousness or flow of words/sounds or sentences in your ear. You may actually feel a sensation around your ears when this happens. Some psychics say they feel a tingling or buzzing or even a ringing before they receive information.

Clairaudient impressions may manifest as a word, an actual phrase, sentence or sound. For example, let's say you lose your keys and can't find them anywhere. You've looked all over the house and then suddenly out of nowhere you hear a voice in your head telling you to look behind the couch. You go behind the couch and boom! The keys are there.

These are a few great exercises to help you develop your clairaudience.

Clairaudience Exercise 1:

Take a few deep breaths and relax your body. Release any tension in your face, shoulders, legs and feet. Now begin to visualize you are going to see the concert of a favorite music artist.

Take a moment to notice where you are seated and how far you are from the stage. Now imagine he/she comes out on and performs one of your favorite songs. Listen to the sounds of the percussion, keyboardist, members of the band playing, pitch/tone of the performer's voice and lyrics of the song. Hear the crowd roar, whistles and cheers in the background.

Take a moment to be there and listen for every sound possible. When you are ready, slowly bring yourself back to the room and open your eyes. Write down any and all sounds you heard including any other observations.

Clairaudience Exercise 2:

Go outside near the park, beach or lake and sit for 5-10 minutes. Close your eyes and listen to the sounds around you. Breathe in the energy of nature and absorb all the sounds. You can also play nature meditation music and focus on particular sounds such as ocean waves, the rainforest or burning firewood.

Clairaudience is a powerful psychic faculty and can assist us not only in intuitive feelings but personal development.

Clairsentience

Clairsentience also known as "clear-knowing" or "clear-feeling" and is described as an inner knowing or sense of something. It's that sixth sense that you just know something but aren't exactly sure how.

Have you ever dated someone and just knew something felt off but you couldn't place your finger on it? This happens all the time unfortunately. We meet someone, date them and through time our intuition tells us maybe this person isn't being completely honest or hiding something.

Clairsentient impressions can also be felt as a gut feeling, intuitive hunch or persistent knowing that won't go away.

Psychically when you practice using your clairsentience the information may come in very quick with strong emotion/feeling or persistent knowing of something.

Practical Clairsentient Exercises

Exercise 1: Close your eyes and take a few deep breaths. Get into a comfortable and relaxed sitting position. Visualize that white light in the core of your stomach expanding connecting you to the universe. As you sit with this light I want you to focus on a concern you would like guidance on. It may be a career question, love or relationship interest or anything you've been contemplating.

Now imagine a Spirit Guide or your Higher Self approaches you with a box. Inside the box are three fortune cookies. Each are of a different color all with a different answer to your concern. There is no right or wrong fortune cookie. Notice the colors of each and feel which one you are drawn to most. Pick one and open it. What does the fortune say? How does the color of the cookie make you feel? Notice any feelings, senses or impressions that may come up as you sit with your fortune.

When you are ready, come back to the room and open your eyes. Now write down what your fortune said and sit with the guidance you just received.

Exercise 2: Close your eyes and take a few deep breaths. Imagine quickly the following elements and notice what feelings/sensations come up when you experience each.

1. Earth.

2. Wind.

3. Fire.

4. Water.

Where are you now? What do you feel? What sensations are you experiencing?

When you are ready, come back to the room and open your eyes. Now write down in your journal your experience. Include any details, sensations, feelings and or visuals.

Clairgustance

Clairgustance is a unique psychic gift and its literal translation is "clear-tasting", the ability to experience taste without the actual presence of anything in the mouth.

When you receive psychic impressions through clairgustance you will feel as if you are tasting something such as food or other substances like cigarettes or alcohol.

For example, you are invited to dinner to meet your significant other's parents for the first time. The dinner reservations are made at an Asian cuisine restaurant. Immediately after you sit down and meet his/her mother and you suddenly get the taste of homemade baked lasagna in your mouth.

Later in conversation, his/her Mom shares that her favorite food is Italian, particularly lasagna. This would be you psychically receiving that information about her with your clairgustance. Pretty fascinating isn't it?

One way to develop your clairgustance is by practicing mindfulness eating.

Exercise: Eat a piece of decadent milk chocolate and instead of swallowing it in one bite, allow it to melt in your mouth, enjoying all the creamy flavors. You can practice this with anything you eat. Notice the textures, flavors and other sensations received by your taste buds.

Clairscent

Clairscent is the last paraphysical sense and means "clear-smelling" which is the ability to perceive smell without the physical presence.

Similar to the other paraphysical senses, clairscent is usually a more subjective experience.

For example, you are house-hunting and tour a fairly new house on the market. You walk into the kitchen and suddenly sense the smell smoke and fire. The realtor tells you there was a small kitchen fire in the house years ago. The actual fire was no longer present but the memory of it was still in the house's energy. You received that information with the clairscent ability.

Exercise: Buy yourself a flower/bouquet of flowers or just walk outside in a park or garden setting. Take in the smells of each flower and breathe in all of the scents. You can also do this with fresh vegetables and herbs.

Chapter 4

T<u>elepathy</u>

Have you ever thought of someone and then at the exact same time or shortly after you receive a call or message from that very person? This is one common experience of telepathy among people.

Telepathy is mind-to-mind communication and is usually much stronger when two individuals share a strong connection. For example, you have probably experienced telepathy with a close best friend or relative. You may say something at the same time or that individual will say exactly what you were thinking.

Some people may say its predictability but I think that as you grow closer with a person your thoughts naturally become in sync and you will pick up on what that person is thinking without them saying a word.

Telepathy is also stronger when the thought or message is emotionally charged rather than just sitting down and trying to send a thought to someone. You will have a higher chance of experiencing telepathy when you are sending an emotionally charged thought or a powerful emotion such as love to someone.

Telepathy can also be experienced when thoughts are shared at the same moment or simultaneously. People may experience this with death. A client of mine woke up in the early morning and sensed her long-distance relative passed away. She checked her phone and received a call confirming the relative had just died.

How can you tell the difference between telepathy and imagination?

Telepathic impressions manifest simultaneously or at the exact same time between two people or as spontaneous information about a person or situation.

Imagination only comes from within and has no connection to reality. It can also manifest as personal wishful thinking or projection towards someone.

When someone mistakes wishful thinking for telepathy, it is because they want their own personal desires or wishes to be expressed or manifested in reality.

Another common mistake for telepathy is projection; where a person puts their own feelings onto someone and believes the other person is experiencing those feelings. People project onto others all the time to avoid taking responsibility for their own actions.

An example of projection confused with telepathy would be a brother who refuses to call his sister after a big argument because he senses she is still mad at him when in reality he is the one who is still angry with her.

Exercise

This exercise is highly recommended to do with a partner either face to face or by phone/Skype. You will also need to set a timer for 15 seconds.

Take a few long deep breaths. Exhale out any tension and clear your mind of any thought. When you are ready, you and your partner will take turns being the sender and the receiver.

The sender will send their partner an emotion for 15 seconds. Don't tell each other what the emotions are. Once time is up the receiver can share what he/she received. The receiver will now be the sender and vice versa. Practice sending each other emotions a few times and then feel free to switch to colors or numbers.

For example, Suzy sets the timer to 15 seconds and sends Jake the emotion "love" in her mind. She concentrates on the feeling and some of her favorite memories of being in love. The timer goes off and Jake shares what he received. They switch being the sender/receiver and now Jake sends Suzy the emotion "anger". He may concentrate on the color red or a scene such as a volcano exploding.

Do this exercise a few times with your partner to build up the momentum and create a stronger telepathic connection. Write down how many times you both got the emotion correct and the sensations, colors or images you received.

Telepathy Exercise #2: Know the Weather & Time

This is a great exercise to practice sensing what the weather or time is throughout the day. Before you begin your day, take a moment to shift your awareness to the weather outside. What do you feel the temperature is or how will it be during the day? Feel free to verify by checking a weather app or the news to see if what you received is accurate.

You can also do this by becoming more mindful of the time. Practice checking your phone or watch less or go an entire day without your watch. Shift your awareness by taking a moment to focus your mind to the energy of the day and see what time pops up in your mind. You can also ask yourself what time it is and then see what your intuition responds with. You may be close to the actual time or pick up on the exact time. Practice this every day and see how well you progress from the beginning of a week to the end.

Chapter 5

Psychometry: Sensing with the Fingers

Psychometry is a powerful psychic tool often described as sensing energy with the fingers. Psychometry literally means "to measure the soul" and is derived from two Greek words, 'psyche' (mind or soul) and 'metron' (to measure).

Merriam-Webster Dictionary defines it as divination of facts concerning an object or its owner through contact with or proximity to the object.

Psychometry is used to sense the auric or energy field around a person, and access information about a place, person, animal or object. Everything, animate and inanimate has an aura or energy field and you can receive information by touching or coming in close contact with it.

Objects, animals, people, locations retain their history in their auric fields. An aura is a life force energy that surrounds every living and nonliving organism. It comes from the Greek word "aura" meaning breeze or breath.

The aura is a light energy usually seen as a light and vibrates around a person, animal or object. It is usually perceived through feeling, sensing or seeing it and psychics will often tune into the auric field of an object with psychometry to access information such as past history and the present.

You may have seen this on television when psychics are asked to help with a missing person case. They will hold an object of the missing person to tune into the energy of the person and receive psychic impressions.

Another example of this is if you have ever walked into a place and received a good or bad vibe about it. You are touching the energy field of this place or person and picking up on the energy.

With psychometry, you can feel the past, receive present information and see possible future circumstances.

Why would you want to use psychometry?

There are plenty of practical uses for psychometry such as finding lost objects like misplacing your keys or wallet. You can also make decisions using it such as deciding on the best product to buy at the store. I do this all the time when I am shopping for household items, groceries or personal items. You can also use it for life changes such as buying a house or car, contract signing, job offers or relocation changes.

You can also find out the history of an object, house or a place using psychometry along with locate missing people or pets.

To practice using psychometry, its best to work with someone's personal object such as a piece of jewelry, cell phone, eyeglasses, a watch or anything metallic. It's better to work with an object that has history versus something brand new. The owner should be able to verify the history of the object for you.

Object Exercise

You will need a personal object or belonging of someone's to practice this exercise such as a cell phone, piece of jewelry or anything they wear frequently.

To practice using psychometry, you need to be in an open and clear mind. Similar to former exercises; take a few deep breaths and hold the object in your left hand while covering it with your right hand. As you hold the object, shift your awareness to the energy of it and notice if any impressions begin to pop in.

You may want to ask questions if you are stuck or not receiving anything. For example, ask in your mind "Was this object a gift or did the owner buy it?", "When did they receive the object?". Notice if any seasons, months or time frames come to you. Look for any emotions, images or sensations.

Write down your impressions and share with the owner what you received.

Photograph Exercise

You can practice the same exercise as above but instead of using an object use a photograph instead. The photograph can be of someone alive or passed and you must be able to verify any details or history about the person. You are welcome to ask for a photograph of someone from a friend or family member or practice on a past historical figure you don't know anything about.

Place the photograph in your left hand and your right hand over it. Take a few deep breaths and focus your energy on the person in the photograph. What sensations or impressions come to you? See if you can locate where the person lived, life of the person, characteristics or demeanor of the individual. See if you can psychometrize the story and background of person. Write down any information that comes to you and then verify how much of what you received was accurate.

Chapter 6

Meditation

There are a variety of methods and tools to help you develop your psychic ability and meditation is one of the most simple and easiest ways to get you started on your spiritual journey.

Meditation can help to still the mind and discover answers to life decisions, tap into inner wisdom and connect with higher vibrational energies such as Spirit Guides. People often think that you need to be a pro at meditating to experience this but actually you don't. There are various ways to meditate from focusing on your breath, mantra meditations or white light meditations.

It can be hard to sit and concentrate on meditating because the mind likes to wander. Some of my clients say meditating is such a difficult task for them. They find themselves distracted by thoughts or end up falling asleep.

In the beginning, it can be very difficult to relax the mind and focus. This process is similar to peeling an onion. You are peeling back layers of junk and mental clutter to get to the core and very essence of yourself.

Patience is especially important in the beginning of your meditation practice. If 15 minutes a day feels too long then focus on 5 minutes a day and gradually increase it. The mind is like a muscle and we need to train it to relax just in the same way we have to physically train our bodies when we exercise. Baby steps are necessary.

If meditation doesn't work for you then I would suggest focusing on a task that is calming or stills your mind. For example, some people say they have the greatest epiphanies while taking a relaxing long hot shower or bath. Sometimes it's cleaning the house, washing dishes, going for a walk or sipping a cup of hot tea.

The following are suggestions to get you started on your meditation journey.

1. Create – It's been often said that our creativity is the doorway to our intuition. In what ways are you creative? Some people enjoy doodling, journaling, painting or just singing in the shower. If you aren't the most creative person, you may be in a way that you aren't even aware of yet.

   Explore your interests in the creative arts. You don't have to be a Picasso to tap into your creative gifts. Just allow yourself the freedom to roam and use your imagination.

2. Spend time in nature- Nature has profound effects on the mind, body and soul. Have you ever just taken a walk in a park and felt so much more at ease after? Being outside whether it's in a local neighborhood park or going to beach will help you become more in touch with your intuition. A clear mind allows us to be open to new discoveries, perspectives and answers. Just by spending time outside and getting some fresh air we are connecting with the Earth and ourselves.

3. Mindfulness – Mindfulness is important with every aspect of our lives. We spend so much time concentrating on the future and what lies ahead that we forget to be here in the now. The next time you go out to dinner or eat a piece of chocolate, spend a few minutes being mindful of the taste, texture and aromas. This exercise will help you connect to the present and savor the experience rather than just passing through it.

4. Solitude – A strong way to tap into our intuition is by spending time with ourselves. Maris Isabel Barreno said "It is only alone; truly alone that one bursts apart, springs forth." In solitude we can listen to our thoughts and wait for the answers. We can talk to God, the Universe, our higher self or whatever divine energy you feel most comfortable connected to.

Spend some with yourself every day for at least 10-15 minutes. You can sit, lie down or relax on the couch. Check in with yourself. How are you feeling? What did you discover today? What has your intuition been telling you and have you been listening? Instead of constantly staying plugged into the outside world, plug into your inner world. Take some much-needed 'me-time'.

Practice using these methods and notice any subtle differences in how you operate in your daily life. Are you more trusting? Are you surrendering to the gut feelings you're receiving. Trust and allow your inner voice to guide you.

Meditation can bring many benefits such as remove emotional blockages, decrease stress, reduce anxiety, increase your ability to concentrate and focus. It may also increase spiritual awareness, open your mind and boost your overall happiness.

Meditation Exercise

Get into a comfortable position and allow your body to relax. Take a few long deep breaths in and exhale. With each exhale, imagine all your tension floating away.

Shift your awareness to your breathing. As you focus on your breath imagine a shimmering pink light at the center of your solar plexus or core of your stomach. This light connects you to a divine energy source, the universe or your higher self.

Imagine it expanding and filling your entire body. As you become more relaxed and safe, allow this light to lead you. Feel your soul take you on a path towards this light to a place of peace and harmony.

Where are you? Perhaps you are near a garden, beach, mountain or an island. Allow yourself to experience any sounds, sights, smells or sensations. Breathe in and feel the energy of this place.

Are there people around or is it just you? Do you see a guide or perhaps your higher self? Sit for a moment and speak with this person or higher version of yourself. Allow the experience to unfold and take you on a journey.

When you are ready you can open your eyes. Write down what you experienced, where you went and who you conversed with. What messages did you receive, if any? How do you feel now versus before the meditation?

You can practice this meditation once a day at the end or the beginning to clear your mind and just relax.

Mantra Meditation

Get into a comfortable position and allow your body to relax. Take a few long deep breaths in and exhale. With each exhale, imagine all your tension floating away.

Shift your awareness to your breathing. As you focus on your breath imagine a golden white light at the center of your solar plexus or core of your stomach. This light connects you to a divine energy source, the universe or your higher self.

Imagine it expanding and filling your entire body. Now take your awareness to your third eye chakra or center of your forehead and repeat the mantra "Om Shanti Om". Om Shanti means "inner peace". Practice repeating this mantra in your mind for at least 5 minutes.

When you are ready, shift your awareness back to the room and open your eyes.

Mantra meditations are useful with concentration, focusing your mind and tuning out other thoughts and distractions.

Focus Exercise

This a simple focus exercise. Get into a relaxed mental state and focus on staring at a candle flame for five minutes.

You can also practice focusing on your breath inhales and exhales or counting numbers backwards by 3s from 100 to 1.

This will help you to shift your mind from your own thoughts to focusing on one task and help to block out any mental distraction.

If you should lose your focus, do the exercise again for as long as you can.

Chapter 7

Symbolism

There are signs and symbols to just about everything in life such as the heart for love, flags for countries, dove for peace and the superstitious black cat for caution. Symbols are used to represent an idea, belief or action for something.

Your intuition will also receive communicate symbols in psychic impressions about a place, person, object or yourself. For example, sometimes when you dream at night you will receive a symbol to communicate an overall theme or aspect of your life such dreaming you are caught in a spider web which could mean you are feeling trapped or stuck.

As you develop your psychic ability, you will receive symbols clairvoyantly or clairaudiently. You may see an image in your mind but aren't sure what the meaning is or how to interpret it. Other times you will just know what the symbol means.

It's very rare that the symbols we receive psychically are literal. Usually symbols are 10% literal and 90% symbolic.

Symbols represent different meanings for each person so when you receive a symbol in a psychic impression, it's subjective and based on your own personal interpretation.

Each psychic's interpretation of a symbol is very different and based on the person's background, belief system and values. Also, one symbol may have many meanings and will change based on the person you read for.

For example, a student of mine was practicing giving a reading to her partner when all she could see was a red telephone booth on the corner of a sidewalk. Immediately her logic thought "London!" and thought her partner may have a connection to London. This would be a literal interpretation. However as we broke it apart, we saw three symbols in this one image.

The color red which she interpreted as love, the telephone booth represented communication and the placement of the telephone booth on the corner meant a crossroads. After she put all her interpretations together she felt this symbol was a representation that her partner was at a crossroads with an intimate relationship and communication concerns.

If someone else received this symbol of a red telephone booth at a crossroad they may have a completely different interpretation. How would you interpret it?

You may see colors, images and symbols when you first meet someone, visit a place, in meditation or in your dreams. For example, you attend a business meeting and the symbol of an engagement ring pops into your mind when your boss addresses everyone. This could mean literally she is engaged or it could represent a new commitment in her life. It's up to you to decide and interpret.

When you receive a symbol there may be strong emotion with it. Pay attention to any feelings or emotions you may sense when you interpret the symbol.

I once saw the symbol of a woman hidden behind a keyhole and felt a strong sense of loneliness and isolation. My partner confirmed her aunt was married to a controlling man who isolated her from the world.

As you work more with your intuition, write down common symbols you receive and create a symbols dictionary. Your subconscious mind will create a database for these symbols along with emotions, colors and feelings associated with them which will become easily accessible to you with time and practice.

There is no right or wrong interpretation of a symbol as this is personal and subjective. You can receive a ton of information in a symbol such as timeframe, personal relationships with family/friends/significant other, personality, interests, job, characteristics, location, age and personal messages.

I remember one of my teachers telling me everything is contained in a symbol. Remember the symbol may not always have the same feelings attached to it and it will change depending on who you are reading for.

Symbols Exercise

You should practice this exercise in a clear and neutral state of mind. Feel free to close your eyes and take a few deep breaths. Relax your body and facial muscles. Shift your awareness to your third eye. As you become aware of your third eye center, focus on any symbols or colors that may appear.

Notice any physical sensations that arise when you see a symbol, subtle feelings or emotions. When you are ready, open your eyes. Write down in your journal what symbols or colors appeared and interpret to the best of your ability.

Tarot Card Exercise

For this exercise you can use a physical deck of tarot cards or search online for images of tarot cards. Pick one tarot card and put it in front of you. Don't look for the meaning of the card just yet.

Get into a meditative state by focusing on your breath and clearing your mind. Take a couple of deep breaths to ground yourself and feel free to surround yourself with the universal white light.

Once you feel relaxed and open, focus your energy on the card and notice what sensations, feelings or symbols appear intuitively.

Write down your impressions and then feel free to compare your impressions with the actual card meaning. Remember even if the card has a specific meaning you can include your own interpretation to it also.

Interpret Symbols Exercise

Concentrate on the following symbols and write down both your literal and subjective interpretation of each.

1. Ocean Waves

2. Golden Retriever Dog

3. Rose

4. A gold watch

5. The color green

Add your interpretations of these symbols to your symbols dictionary and use them for reference when necessary.

Chapter 8

Dreams

One of the most common ways for us to tap into our intuition is through our dreams. In our dreams we are able to better connect with our subconscious mind for information about our emotional, psychological and mental state. We can work through emotional clutter, life concerns and past issues in the dream state. In our dreams, we can also heal and release buried anger, sadness or resentment towards a situation or person.

Intuitively, our dreams can also work with us to communicate powerful psychic messages, symbols and premonitions. Dreams are a direct line to our higher selves, soul wisdom, Spirit and this unique invisible world that we can't always feel in our waking state.

We may be so busy with life responsibilities during the day that it may be nearly impossible to hear or listen to our intuition or pay attention to psychic impressions that may be received. These impressions will be subconsciously remembered and then communicated to us in our dream state later.

Have you ever had a dream about a relative or close friend with specific information about their life and later it came true? This has happened to me more times than I can count.

This also can happen when you share a deep bond or connection with someone. You may start to receive psychic impressions about him/her in your sleep.

For example, I am very close with my cousin Diana. If we haven't spoken in a while I will have dreams about her life including new changes, current emotional state or overall life concerns. We share a strong telepathic connection and will often communicate with each other in our dream states.

Dreams can also communicate information about the future such as premonitions or information about the past.

An example of this is a client of mine had reoccurring dreams she was going to move from New York to California. Yet at the time she wasn't looking for a new job or interested in moving. Six months later she fell in love with a man from California and decided to relocate for the relationship and a job opportunity.

You may also receive on past and present information about someone in your dreams. Have you ever met someone or started dating a new person and then had vivid dream about them? One client told me about a reoccurring dream about a new love interest regarding secrecy and deception. Months later she found out he was married and having an affair on his wife with her.

Dreams can communicate positive and negative messages to us about ourselves, people we know and life in general.

Personally, I love to dream. It's one of the reasons I look forward to falling asleep at night. In the beginning of my psychic development my dreams were the doorway to my intuition and Spirit communication. They still are but in a different way. Usually in the beginning when you start to become more aware you will have more vivid intuitive dreams about the past, present or the future.

You are subconsciously working in your sleep to tap into your psychic ability. You may also communicate with passed loved ones or Spirit Guides in your dreams. I have many clients including myself who communicate with the deceased or a guide in the dream state.

Why would the deceased want to communicate with us after they pass? One reason is to let us know they are okay and still around us bringing comfort. Another reason is to provide guidance or information on current issues. A common dream I've noticed people have about passed loved ones is only seeing their face and nothing else. This is usually a sign from them letting you know they are around you and sending you a little hello.

You may also receive symbols and numbers in your dreams. If you aren't able to interpret the meaning behind them, write it down for reference later or research what the number means. I would highly suggest keeping a dream journal or recording your dreams in your phone or any audio-recording device. A dream journal will help document specific dreams, messages you receive or patterns of themes and symbols.

If you are still perplexed by a symbol received in a dream then I would recommend looking at some books on symbols and their meanings.

Dream Exercise

One common bedtime dream exercise to do is write down a question or concern you'd like guidance on. An example of this would be a question focused on career such as "Is this job right for me?".

Focus on that question and read it in your mind a few times while concentrating on receiving guidance about it. Then say in your mind, "When I wake up tomorrow I will remember all of my dreams."

This exercise may work immediately or it may take a few rounds of practice to receive anything. If you don't receive an answer but see something instead, write it down and keep practicing every night. You can also buy a crystal specifically for dreams and putting that under your pillow before bed.

Chapter 9

Your Spiritual Journey

"We are not human beings having a spiritual experience. We are spiritual beings having a human experience." -Pierre Teilhard de Chardin

As you grow and explore these psychic gifts, you will expand not only as a human but as a spiritual being. In my own personal experience, I feel as though I have tapped into a certain magic that never existed before.

Life challenges and difficulties will still exist but the way in which you perceive them will shift. As long as you practice trusting your psychic impressions and listening to your intuition you will slowly see a radical change in yourself and in the world around you.

People may also see you differently because as you change and grow within so does the world outside of you. Not everyone's purpose is to be a professional psychic or a medium but developing your intuition and psychic gifts are the foundation to finding your soul purpose on this Earth.

It is said that Earth is our temporary home until we actually return back to our real home so while we are here we should try to make the best of it. We come here to learn specific lessons and clear karmic debts and grow spiritually.

Your intuition will serve as a compass to the life you live and the purpose you are here to fulfill. We all play a special role in the overall cosmic consciousness of humanity.

Be kind and allow your intuition to be your guide not only to help yourself but to help others. You can be a true inspiration for your family and friends and anyone who meets you.

There may be skeptics and people who doubt exploring this gift of intuition but remember that nothing is meant to be taken personally. We all have own baggage and it's important to just stand firm in your own light.

You are magic. You are pure existence.

Wherever you go in your journey it is yours to decide.

Developing your psychic gifts are just one small piece of the pie. There is the healing arts and various therapies. I've had students come in for my class and have continued on to become Reiki practitioners, hypnotherapists, mediums and some just enjoy learning the information and practicing it in their own life.

Be open to all possibilities and don't put restrictions on yourself or what you are capable of doing. Psychic ability is something to be used and practiced with for higher purposes of positivity and good.

Intuition will always be there as that little voice guiding you in times of darkness and light. It's there to help you become the best version of yourself and live the most fulfilled human experience possible.

Free Downloads

Download a Free iTunes Psychic Development Podcast by Emily

Afterword_

It's been a wonderful journey writing this book and sharing the knowledge of my development with you. I thank you for being a part of this with me and for taking the time to read it. I hope that it not only helps you on your journey but opens you to a whole new world as it has for me.

You will grow, expand and change spiritually. I have changed so much since the beginning of my journey. At times, I doubted my abilities and questioned my purpose and if this work was really meant for me. However one thing I've learned is that you can't hide from yourself.

No matter how much I doubted myself something kept pushing me to go further, deeper and rise above my own insecurities and fears with being a psychic medium.

Discovering your purpose is like a fingerprint, unique only to you. Timing is everything.

The more work we do on ourselves the stronger and more sensitive we become to our psychic ability. Allow yourself to heal from past wounds, old hurts and fight through fears and doubts.

There is so much we can give to each other and ourselves. Pay attention to the synchronicities and signs. Magic is everywhere if we just allow ourselves to open up and see it.

I will be publishing a second book on Mediumship for Beginners covering all aspects of mediumship along with exercises on how to connect with Spirit, Spirit Guides and understanding how they communicate with us. I thank you for your support and interest in my writing and I look forward to hearing from you in the future.

You can always contact me via my website, www.emilystroia.com to book a private reading or to sign up for my psychic development classes.

Thank you and Namaste!

About Emily

Emily Stroia is a professional Intuitive and Medium based in the New York City metro and New Jersey area. She uses her intuition and mediumship abilities to offer guidance to all her clients, encouraging them to move forward in a positive direction no matter what obstacles the future has in store for them. She also updates a personal blog and teaches classes on developing your intuitive and spiritual gifts.

Currently, Emily lives in the greater NYC area and offers psychic readings by appointment only via in Person, Skype or Phone. To learn more about Emily, visit www.emilystroia.com

Made in the USA
Las Vegas, NV
17 October 2024

97037804R00030